This book is dedicated to my husband. Without his encouragement it would probably still be saved on our laptop and would have remained a dream. To my wonderful boys Nathan, the prospect of your mother becoming an author fascinated you so much it drove me to complete this book, and Ryan, your faith in God is a gift. Thank you for praying for mummy's book.

In loving memory of my Dad. I now understand why you believed in me so much, for I can see myself through your eyes. Thank you for instilling in me the belief that I can achieve anything. This one is for you.

Gertrude Nyirenda

Acknowledgements

To God, the author of my life. All Glory and Honour belongs to you. Thank you for the inspiration.

Epi Mabika, my Publishing Consultant, without your intervention I would not have managed to complete this book. It has been a life changing experience for me. You have a great work ethic and your standard of excellence is matchless! I still can't believe you managed to push this book out of me in 90 days. Thank you.

My Family: My mum, Maria Fatima; my siblings - Eunice, Irene, Lovemore and Gladmore. Your love and support has helped me achieve my dreams. I'm forever grateful.

Monika Wojtowicz, our coffee mornings at Starbucks were not in vain. You taught me that I only have one life to live so I should live it and follow my dreams, I took your advice.

Gertrude Nyirenda

Weight Loss Wars

My Journey to health, happiness and beyond.

By

Gertrude Nyirenda

www.fast-print.net/store.php

WEIGHT LOSS WARS

A catalogue record for this book is available from the British Library

ISBN 978-178456-148-2

First published 2015 by
FASTPRINT PUBLISHING
Peterborough, England.

'Weight Loss Wars'

Is also available as an audio
book and digital e-book.

More copies can be ordered
at**www.weightlosswars.co.uk**

and

www.amazon.com
and all good book stores.

Contents

Foreword

Having struggled with weight loss for seventeen years, could I have found the secret to successful weight loss and with it my destiny?

Weight Loss Wars was written after an extensive research and study of various diets and exercise programmes, all condensed into one plan that truly succeeded. In the book, you will discover that weight Loss can be a journey to enjoy and is not a boring task to endure. It's not about dieting or overly restricting your food intake, or cutting out your favourite food, but rather weight loss, can be a journey of discovering the real you, falling in love with yourself both inside and out, through changing your lifestyle whilst enjoying it.

Earl Nightingale once stated, "We are our very best and happiest when we are fully engaged in work we enjoy, on the journey toward the goal we've established for ourselves. It gives meaning to our time off and comfort to our sleep. It makes everything else in life so wonderful so worthwhile".

You will discover that you can have a healthy relationship with food and exercise whilst enjoying losing weight. You will fall in love with something that truly excites you, while challenging you to take total control of your weight loss. Have you ever wondered why diets don't seem to work? Well your questions to why diets don't work for someone who has a lot of weight to lose and wants to keep the weight off for good will be answered in this book.

You will also get my personalised 26 key secrets entitled *The ABC Guide*, to help kick start your own weight loss journey, together with tips on keeping it exciting and not want to give up on your journey before you reach your ideal weight goal. I applied all these to my journey and was successful in achieving my ideal weight.

Preface

The Big 'O'

Overweight is defined in the *Oxford Dictionary* quite simply as 'of a thing: above, or in excess of a specified, allowed, or suitable weight; too heavy. The National Health Service in England defines it as a term that is used to describe someone who is above a weight considered normal or desirable, or simply someone with a lot of body fat.

A person is usually overweight before they become obese, so a person can be overweight without being obese. Measurement of Weight is usually based on your 'Body Mass Index' (BMI is a measure used to gauge obesity) which you can check using a BMI calculator. BMI equates your weight to your height, age, sex, and it will come up with a figure representing what is known as your BMI. If your BMI is in the range 25 to 29 then you are not at a healthy weight and will be considered to be overweight, which will eventually lead to obesity. The BMI is a good estimate of how much fat is in your body.

The main cause of being overweight or obese is generally consuming more calories than your body needs. The excess energy is then stored in the body as fat.

Being overweight is a common problem in the United Kingdom and according to the head of the NHS in England; it is the 'new smoking' in terms of its impact on health and the cost to the NHS. The problem is estimated to cost the NHS £9 billion a year, and if it continues to rise it will threaten the sustainability of the health service.

Being overweight is estimated to affect around one in every four adults.

Researchers see global weight gain as a bigger threat to mankind than population growth. They are concerned not only about the health implications but the environmental impact as well. Increasing obesity could have the same impact on global resources as an extra billion people.

Someone might argue that there is nothing wrong with being overweight. We are all entitled to our opinion, and there is no right or wrong in the way you look. My motto is if you like the way you look then there is no problem. The only argument I would put across is, excess body weight does not only affect image issues, but your health is also at risk. Ezra Taft Benson stated that, "You are free to choose, but you are not free from the consequences of your choice". If you are overweight, you might have an increased risk of developing the following diseases:

Type Two Diabetes is a lifelong condition that causes a person's blood sugar level to become too high. It occurs when the body doesn't produce enough insulin to function properly, or when the body cells do not react to insulin. According to the NHS website, the leading cause of 'type two diabetes' is obesity. In England in 2010 there were approximately 3.1 million people aged over 16 with diabetes. By 2030, this figure is expected to rise to 4.6 million, which is 90 per cent of all adults in England. Excess fat makes your body resistant to insulin. When this happens your cells cannot get the energy they need.

Hypertension, also known as high blood pressure is when the pressure of the blood in your arteries (an artery is a tube that carries the blood in your body from your heart to your brain) is consistently higher than the recommended level. If you have high blood pressure, this higher pressure puts extra strain on your heart and blood vessels, which could eventually lead to a heart attack or stroke. Overweight individuals have an increase in fatty tissue that increases their vascular resistance and in turn increase the work the heart has to do to pump blood throughout the body.

Breathing Problems, when you gain weight and do not exercise regularly you may experience shortness of breath quiet easily. Excess fat restricts the expansion of the rib cage and leaves less space for the diaphragm to move downwards as it should.

Cancer, a new study shows that eating healthy and daily walking can cut the risk of cancer. Evidence is growing that physical activity is crucial in protecting against cancer recurrence and death. For cancer patients, physical activity does not only reduce the risk of dying or the cancer coming back, it can also help manage some of the devastating side effects of treatment, such as fatigue or anxiety, this is according to a report by Ciaran Devane, from Macmillan Cancer Support. Professor Jane Maher commented in the *Daily Mirror* that every year in the UK, hundreds of millions of pounds are spent on drugs to help prevent and treat cancer, yet walking just a mile per day can help cancer patients to reduce their risk of dying from the disease. She then proceeded to comment that she regularly recommends physical activity to patients and she is convinced about the health benefits of keeping active.

The NHS to help tackle the big 'O' offers a range of services such as

- Free local weight loss groups for one year, which would coincide with a free gym membership.
- Exercise on prescription, this is where you are referred to a local active health team for a number of sessions with a qualified trainer supervising you.
- Help with making healthier food choices and physical activity through the 'Change for life Programme', which is readily available on the Internet.
- Improving of labelling on food and drink to help people make informed healthier choices.
- Guidance is also being given on how much physical activity an individual needs on a daily basis.
- The government is also encouraging responsible business through the 'Public Health Responsibility Deal' to make it easier for everyone from members of staff in companies to their customers, to make healthier eating choices.
- One of the new proposal's that is being currently discussed is whether more money should be invested into lifestyle change intervention programmes rather

than the current bariatric surgery for obese patients.

- Another option under consideration is giving local councils extra powers to make local decisions about issues such as fast food, alcohol and tobacco, to try and curb the huge increase in Obesity.

The only healthy way to tackle the Big 'O' is to develop a *healthy lifestyle* and gradually lose weight through a combination of eating a low calorie diet, which consists of all of your five a day – plenty of fruit and vegetables – some milk and dairy products and regular exercise. Avoid foods that contain high levels of salt and eventually be able to maintain that weight loss.

Introduction

My Weight Loss Journey

So here I am 35 years old, married to a loving husband who supports me in everything I decide to do. Blessed with two wonderful boys who keep me very busy, the joys of being a mum, what more could I ask for right…?

Well that is where *Weight Loss Wars*, my journey was birthed. Rewind a few years back, I had come to a point in my life when I felt hopeless and frustrated; I had not achieved anything in my life. I had attempted to study a nursing course, but I was diagnosed with sciatica, a type of excruciating pain caused by the sciatic nerve being irritated or compressed. The sciatic nerve is the longest nerve in the body, which runs from the pelvis through the buttock area down to the legs and feet. That dashed my hopes and dreams of pursuing a career in nursing. I even tried studying a Theology Degree - too much work, so I gave up.

Through all these emotions, one of Albert Einstein's famous quotes motivated me, he once said, "Everybody is a genius". But if you judge a fish by its ability to climb a tree, it will live its whole life believing that it is stupid". So I knew I was not stupid, I just had to find the right career path, one that suited me.

I still felt like a complete failure, I had no degree or career, to make it worse, I felt trapped in the job where I was working at that time. The worst part was; I didn't even have an idea of what I wanted to do with my life. Michel de Montaigne summed up my feelings when he said that, "I know well what I am fleeing from but not what I am in search of". Not that I was not grateful for the all the other beautiful things in my life I had been blessed with, like my family.

Still I yearned for something that was personal to me and that I could have achieved as an individual. There had to be something better out there for me. I was convinced that the reason I felt that there was something better out there in terms of a career, or as I like to call it a source of income, was because there was. There had to be, and of this I was certain!

There was a burning desire to birth something I felt was hiding way deep inside, waiting to emerge. How could I help that feeling when I didn't even know myself what that something was? All I knew was I had a reason and a purpose for being born, I wanted to help people maximise their potential, live a more fulfilled life by changing their lives, but of course I had to start with me.

So I began searching and it was while on one of my countless searches, in the quest to fulfil this burning desire of a better me that I came across a book written by Neale Donald Walsch entitled

Conversations with God. The title caught my attention and I began searching for the book online. Unfortunately I never actually got to read the book, I hope to read it someday, maybe even meet Donald Walsch in person. However, I managed to watch a video clip on the Internet about how he came to write his book.

Something big and amazing was birthed at the lowest point in Neales life (his book). He had been divorced four times, was out of a job and had just recently been involved in a car accident and broken his neck. To add to all that he was homeless. Neale had a lot of questions about the way his life had turned out, and wanted someone to answer them. Despondent, he began his writings, consisting of questions and the answers to those questions of why his life had ended up the way it had. His first book became an international bestseller.

Not that my life was as dramatic as Neale Donald Walsch's, but all of my fears and failures, my insecurities, were reflected in this film. I was greatly inspired by his story. This gave me an idea to also write a book about my journey through life, especially my weight loss. To write about the one area in my life where I had taken total control of a problem I had battled with for years and finally, I had experienced a complete and total sweet victory.

Having lost more than six stone (nearly 40 kg), the healthy way, was a life changing experience for me. If I could do it, then anyone could. I wanted to encourage anyone who was trying to lose weight to face it head on, and take responsibility for their own happiness.

Most importantly, I just simply wanted to tell you how I did it. I could let you be inspired by how I dealt with my imperfections through an inspirational, intimate and emotional story covering seventeen years of one area I had struggled with; my weight. But it just does not centre on weight loss, anyone can identify with it. It will take you on a journey showing you that what I had perceived to be ashes and ruins in my life, ranging from being overweight, rejection and bulimia, until eventually discovering something beautiful from those ashes. The battle of losing weight is what won the war for me, and turned out to be the key that would unlock my destiny.

Maybe you are not struggling with weight loss, but whatever you are facing today, *Weight Loss Wars* will take you on a roller coaster of emotions ranging from anger, love, fear, to experiencing pure joy, in the journey to discovering yourself and realising that there is no greater satisfaction that can compare with realising that even the mistakes you made in your life, and the misfortunes all helped to shape and mould your destiny.

This book will inspire you to turn your life around by perceiving your situation differently. The mind is a powerful tool, every decision and action we make starts in the mind.

I wanted to share my journey with the world in singer Emeli Sande's words;

"I wanna sing,
I wanna shout,
I want to scream till the words dry out of my mouth,
So put it in all of the papers,
I'm not afraid.
They can read all about it"...

And in turn, I will offer you my lenses to view yourself differently and take the necessary steps that you need to follow your dreams by moulding yourself into the character you long to be. James A. Froude quoted it well when he said, 'you cannot dream yourself into a character. You must hammer and forge yourself into one'.

Chapter One

Growing Up

Looking back at my childhood, it is not hard to see why I had become overweight; the answer was simply that I loved food. I loved it when I was happy, I loved it when I was sad, so I wasn't a comfort eater, nor did I need an excuse to eat, I just loved food.

I have always suffered with what I like to term as a 'food addiction'. Having grown up in the southern part of Africa, where it is predominately populated by African people who believe that when you serve your family large amounts of food, it is perceived as a sign of being very wealthy. Why not? If you have it flaunt it, right? The only problem is serving large portion of food leads to being overweight and causes various other diseases. A lesson I learnt late in life.

So food was a happy part of my life, my childhood friend Elsa and I would often hold food-tasting sessions, where we would try out new recipes and spend a whole afternoon dedicated to describing the different, distinctive and delectable scrumptious flavours of whatever we were eating. Eating made me feel happy.

My mother was not very helpful either, bless her, she too had a love for food, and was very generous, offering large helpings of her hearty cooked meals and there was always a big dollop of mayonnaise to complement her food. I never could understand why, but I gladly embraced the culture in our home. Yes my mum was known for her love for mayonnaise, my dad would often joke that after shopping if there wasn't a jar of mayonnaise in the shopping trolley, then my mum's shopping wasn't complete. Food was always within easy reach in our home when I was young. It was the only thing you wouldn't get told off for taking without permission.

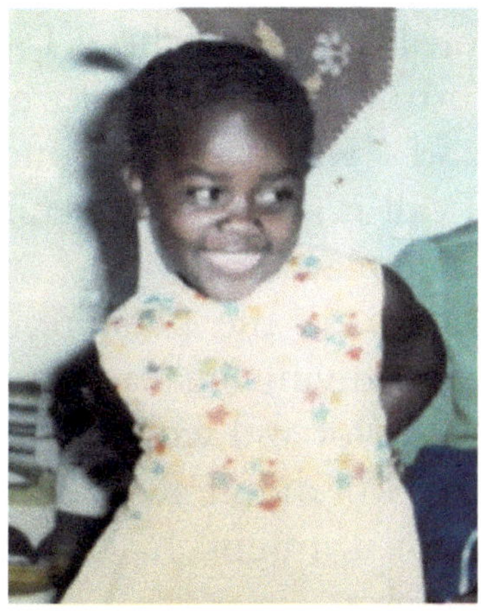

Here is a photo of me at age four.

That explains why I have always struggled with my weight. My Elder sister Eunice even had a nickname for me; I often wonder if she still remembers, 'Dudes' translated "little fat person". I remember being called 'fat cook' at school. A song was even composed in my honour, 'Duuuuff Duna' which simply translates to "a very fat person".

The way I looked and being made fun of, never really bothered me at all. I was a little chubby, but I loved it, even my earlobes where chubby.

Miraculously in high school I lost all the baby fat, but unfortunately, not my love for food. Now I understand why this wonderful miracle occurred. I call it a wonderful miracle because at school, I never played any sport, as I did not like anything that made me perspire, so I opted for swimming and diving instead, but then suffered with tonsillitis a lot and would often be signed off by the doctor. So I didn't swim as often as I would have loved to. I might have become the next Rebecca Adlington.

But anyway this wonderful miracle happened, because you see on my fourteenth birthday my late dad – may his soul rest in peace – bought me a bicycle, so I used to cycle to and from school, a form of exercise, ahhhh! Another very valuable lesson I learnt late in life. The cycling to and from school contributed to my weight loss, so I had no weight issues until I turned seventeen. That is when my weight problems came back.

I grew up in Bulawayo, the second largest, very beautiful sunshine city in Zimbabwe, which can be found in the southern part of Africa. The way the system worked in Zimbabwe at the time I was growing up was that at the age of sixteen, you had to sit national exams known as 'Ordinary Levels', equivalent to GCSE in England, and after these exams you stay at home for a good four months waiting for your results.

As you might have guessed, I was at home for four months, after sitting my Ordinary Levels. I desperately needed to find something to amuse myself. Well yes I turned to my favourite hobby, snacking on cake, crisps and my favourite pork pie, washed down with a bottle of nice ice-cold Cream Soda. It was heaven. All that snacking, and coupled with no exercise because my bicycle was left to gather dust in our garage. It was oblivious to me that the cycling was what had kept me at a healthy weight, so yes the pounds piled on.

Since no one in my family mentioned it, or maybe they did not notice it. I continued with my eating escapades. Even though I noticed that I had piled on a few pounds and was floating round like a balloon, I convinced myself that I could easily lose the weight when I was ready. But when I went to college, my bad eating habits escalated. Right opposite our college was a bakery, come on; they baked fresh samosas and delicious meat pies that called to me every morning. Who needed to carry a healthy packed lunch from home? Certainly not me! Besides healthy was not practiced in our home. For a whole three years I ate to my heart's content and still my weight rose steadily and unnoticed by the rest of my family.

Until the day my family and I went to visit my late uncle Robson. Now, uncle Robson had an obsession with mirrors. Put lightly, he had a very big house, and almost all the walls in every room were covered with mirrors.

Unfortunately for me, he had a very large mirror in the corridor, and as I walked past it, I caught a glimpse of this humongous teenage girl staring back at me. I did not recognise myself at all, apart from the clothes I was wearing and the big beautiful eyes God blessed me with, which were staring back at me in total amazement.

Oh my God, it was me. How had I allowed myself to get like this? The rest of that evening is but a distant memory. I do not recall much of what happened that evening, nor do I have a desire to remember, all I know is it was one of my lowest moments.

So in July 1998 – I have no recollection of the exact date – I had my first real experience of what being overweight looked like. I do however vividly remember the month, because that same month, my sweet grandmother went to be with the Lord, at the age of seventy-one. So not only did I lose my grandmother, whom I loved and cherished dearly, that's the same year I also tasted the bitter feeling of being overweight. I felt so ashamed. The horrid image of the fat person I had seen staring back at me the previous night was embedded in my memory. I did not know who to turn to, to discuss that person I had seen staring back at me in the mirror the previous night. However it bothered terribly.

All I knew was I had to lose weight and fast. I set out on a mission to lose weight, with no knowledge of healthy eating and exercise. All I knew was I had to kiss my love of food goodbye, as they say it's a thin line between love and hate, but to me that was the only solution.

The only person I felt I could turn to and seek help from, was our housemaid whom was employed by my parents at that time. Seriously I can't help but laugh at myself now because she herself was overweight. But anyway I ignorantly enquired from her if she knew of ways I could lose weight and fast. She hesitantly suggested slimming tablets and laxatives.

Wow! To me that sounded like a very good idea. I had heard some of my friends talking about slimming tables and how they had helped them to lose their appetite. That sounded like the perfect solution, so I decided they would be safe to try.

The following morning, I headed to the pharmacy. Unfortunately they did not have any slimming tablets in stock that day. What a dilemma, I could not afford to wait another day. I quickly remembered that my housemaid had also mentioned laxatives, so I went ahead and asked if they had any laxatives instead. My question worried the pharmacist, so she asked me what I needed the laxatives for. Without even stopping to think about it, the lies just rolled off my tongue, and I answered her that I had been feeling constipated of late. Thank goodness she believed my innocent looking face and sold me the laxatives.

I could not wait to get home and try them out, which of cause was a very big mistake, total disaster, which I definitely lived to regret. On the first night I took the laxatives, the whole family had to travel a six-hour journey to Harare, the capital city in Zimbabwe to attend my late grandmother's funeral. I will leave the results of my having taken that laxative to your imagination. I vowed never to take another laxative again.

My weight issues were put on hold for a whole weekend while I mourned my late grandmother. Lucky for me I was too upset to eat anyway. But as soon as we got back to Bulawayo, my quest continued.

First I had to find out how much I weighed, so I went back to the pharmacy paid my 20 cents, and I weighed in at 68Kg, (10 stone 12 pounds), which was overweight for my little frame. So I came up with the perfect solution; I hated food, it was because of food I had ended up like this. To make matters worse, there were two very important occasions coming up, it was vital to get a solution fast. Both my sister's where getting married and I was a bridesmaid in both weddings. Irene had even asked me to be her maid of honour. She must have been blind. What a dilemma.

Since I had lived to regret taking the laxatives, an experience I will never forget, the only solution was to starve myself, yes to starve myself. I would only eat to survive. Carefully I thought about the one thing I could not live without eating... Steak bake, looking back it didn't take much to please me, I still love a steak bake now specially from 'The Wild Bean Café'; it's to die for. Every bite will satisfy you, urging and encouraging you to take another bite.

So all I ate was a steak bake for lunch, or if I fancied something different, I would have a doughnut instead. I would have no breakfast and no dinner, I hid it well from the rest of my family, and for sure the pounds starting to fall off.

The hunger pangs were to serve as a reminder that if I ate I would end up fat again. I wanted to feel those hunger pangs, I thrived on them. Sure enough, I managed to lose a good 8kgs, (1 stone 3 pounds).

Chapter Two

Eating Disorders

Starving myself didn't work out well in the end, it proved disastrous, it had been a few months of starving myself and I could not keep my energy levels up any longer, I felt tired all the time, but worst of all, I terribly missed my first love, (food).

That's when the nightmares began; eating had worked its way into my dreams. Often, I would have nightmares of me eating all of my favourite foods. I had to think of another solution fast. The last thing I wanted was to be overweight again. That image of that humongous girl staring back at me in the mirror had traumatised me.

So I came up with another bright idea, good thing I had paid attention in Biology class, I thought to myself what if the times when I could not bear the hunger pangs, I would eat all I wanted to my heart's content, then make myself sick afterwards, this way the food would not get digested, so I would not end up fat again. This seemed like a brilliant plan. I was a foolish genius.

So once again I consulted our housemaid, and she advised me to drink lots of fluids to moisten the food, so it wouldn't be so uncomfortable wrenching my heart out. I took her advice on board, and it sure did help.

That's what I did; I became bulimic, though at the time I didn't even know that it was actually an eating disorder. It was not as well documented as it is now. I've since discovered that Bulimia Nervosa is an eating disorder that affects not only teenagers but adults as well. In the United Kingdom alone there are estimated to be approximately 165,000 cases. It has a higher death rate than any other psychiatric disorder, according to the Eating Disorders Association.

People who suffer from this eating disorder have a real fear of weight gain, and they usually have a distorted view of their body size and shape. They try and control their weight by severely restricting the amount of food they eat, or when they do eat, they make themselves vomit, sometimes violently, because they feel guilty and often fear that they will get fat from the food they have eaten. It is more than just going on a diet or trying to lose weight, it is more extreme. That perfectly described me, except I did not have a distorted view of my body size and shape, I actually was overweight. Bulimia Nervosa sadly has a twin called Anorexia Nervosa, which is an eating disorder characterised by an obsessive desire to lose weight by refusing to eat.

That is what I resorted to, in my ignorance, I would enjoy whatever food I wanted, and then stick my fingers down my throat to inflict self-induced vomiting. It was horrible, it tasted disgusting, but then I would envision the fat girl staring back at me in the mirror. So with tears running down my cheeks, I would make myself vomit.

I'm the one on the left hand side.

Once that disgusting ordeal was over it didn't seem so bad, I had the perfect body I wanted. Surely it wouldn't hurt, or, would it? So I worked on my new brilliant idea, which seemed to work at that time, my weight was dropping and fast. The months went by. This was the result. But what a high price I had to pay. Yes I looked fabulous at my sister Eunice's wedding.

And at Irene's wedding

Yes, a beautiful slim Gertrude. I continued to self-harm for several months and I managed to deceive my family. Everything was going really well, I managed to deceive myself that I had the best of both worlds, eat all I want and still have the body I loved. That was until I developed a peptic ulcer. That is one of the complications you get from bulimia nervosa, you see the gastric juices from my stomach were slowly eroding the lining of my stomach, this was happening every time I made myself sick, I was self-harming and was oblivious to this fact, until my whole stomach was racked with pain it was unbearable, I would often pass out from the pain. I had literally damaged part of my digestive system.

I was fortunate that was the only complication I got from the few months I had violently made myself vomit. Other medical complications include, rotting teeth, gingivitis which is inflammation of the gum tissue, heart failure, inflammation of the esophagus, swelling of glands near the cheeks, and dehydration. Just to mention a few as there are a lot more damaging side-effects.

I am very lucky to have walked away with just one complication, but I paid dearly for it. I was vomiting all the time after every meal, bringing up bile, which was yellowish in colour. On one occasion my sister Irene had to rush me to hospital. It got so bad that I had to be admitted into hospital for a whole week, while they carried out tests on me to find out what was causing all the vomiting and abdominal pain.

My poor dad had no idea what was going on. I recall the doctor saying to him, 'Mr Shana, it appears your daughter has developed a peptic ulcer and it looks like it's going to perforate. If she continues like this we might need to operate on her to see what's going on inside her stomach'. I did not understand those medical terms and jargon such as perforate and ulcer, but I was clever enough to know that it did not sound good and I knew exactly what had caused them.

My heart galloped in my ears, as deep fear and anxiety seized me, paralysing my whole body. I was torn between telling the doctor the truth about my little secret and keeping it to myself... but, what if he told my dad? I could not bear to disappoint my dad. He always had very high expectations of me.

So I decided to play along and not know the cause of all this pain wrenching through my stomach, which I found very draining, I just wanted it to end…

The doctor's words echoed in my ears, overtaking the sound of my galloping heart. I can still hear those words echoing in my ears today, as if it was yesterday. At that point, the whole room turned so dark it was as if two midnights had been put together. A sharp pain racked across my abdomen, and I felt myself slipping away slowly. I'm sure I must have passed out from the severity of the pain, because all I remember after what seemed like a very long time, is opening my eyes to find my dad siting on the chair beside me, tears streaming down his cheeks, he quickly turned away so that I would not see him crying.

That broke my heart into a thousand pieces, as the severity of what I had done to myself suddenly dawned on me. My dad loved all his five children to bits, he would have moved heaven and earth for my brothers, sisters and I if he could, and in fact he did on a countless number of occasions and this was how I had repaid him. What sheer disappointment.

Looking at him and knowing I had caused not only him, but myself also so much heartache and pain. I made a decision that minute, I remember instantly saying a little prayer and asking God to heal me, I made a promise to myself never to stick my fingers down my throat to make myself sick ever again. Nothing was worth all this suffering. I knew exactly how to stop all this pain from coming back.

I was in hospital for the rest of that week and found it very lonely and boring, apart from the fuss everyone was making around me, I really did not want to be there. The day I was discharged and allowed to go home, was a new turning point. I was determined never to make myself sick again; I had paid a very high price, which had left an imprint on my brain, and an ulcer I had to live with for the rest of my life. Besides, I was determined to never go back into that hospital again; the food was horrible. So I learned to get better myself, I started eating normally again. It's comforting to know that with help, the effects of any eating disorders can be treated, leaving the body to heal and return to normal. However, if left untreated for years, the effects of an eating disorder can be life threatening and irreversible.

Considering I had been bulimic for two years, I managed to recover quite quickly; sadly I still suffer from ulcer pain today. I guess it serves as a reminder that I never want to be bulimic ever again. Bulimia was a closed chapter in my life, never to be revisited.

So I kissed it goodbye and we parted ways. I returned to my normal eating habits, sub consciously I must have been eating healthy, because even though I gradually put on weight, the ironic thing is I put on just the one stone 2 pounds (8kgs), which is exactly what I had lost while I was bulimic and managed to maintain that weight for nearly three years.

Chapter Three

Return of the Weight Loss Demons

In September 1999, I migrated to The United Kingdom, and on my second day of being in England I met the love of my life Ko Nyirenda. I'm not ashamed to admit that it was love at first site on my part. I knew I loved him instantly the day I met him.

Within days of meeting one other we were inseparable. I remember looking at his very attractive unlined face and thinking he had the kindest eyes I had ever seen. I often got lost just staring into those eyes and the warmest smile, which melted away any doubts I might have had about him. As destiny would have it, fate took over and we were married two years later on 28 April 2001. I was a stunning bride. My wedding dress was a slender size 10. By this time I was 23 years old, I had miraculously maintained the same weight, which was just about a healthy weight for my body frame and I managed to maintain this weight without being cautious of my eating habits and exercise.

I must have adapted to my new life in the UK quite well. Though life in the UK was different however, food was still within easy reach, the modern lifestyle appeared to encourage eating excessive amounts of food that were high in calories and often contained large amounts of sugar. You didn't and still don't have to look very hard to find a MacDonald's or Kentucky Fried Chicken. But I was loving it. These fast foods, sweets and chocolates often cost less than the healthy options that were available, which was a bonus being on the minimum wage. I particularly fell in love with the big adverts reading 'buy one get one free'. Wow!

That's me on my wedding day.

Though I had a different approach to food, it all still lead to obesity. I didn't eat pasties as often as I did when I was in Zimbabwe, but I soon found substitutes. I welcomed them all. There were sweets around every corner. Come Christmas time, everyone gave you a box of chocolates, with a variety to choose from, there were Celebrations, Quality Street, and all these were given to you as presents. For the first time in my life I couldn't eat all the chocolates I had been given. I even managed to give some away. There was no chance to miss the pork pies I had often indulged in.

Nevertheless, my weight demons were a distant memory, long forgotten. Oblivious to the fact that the pounds were piling on, I continued to indulge in my favourite food; cheddar biscuits soon became one of my favourites as well.

Whilst carrying out my eating escapades, the weight demons never seemed to bother me, they only returned to haunt me after I gave birth to my eldest son Nathan Sean.

Looking back now, I can see that I encouraged them and welcomed them back with wide-open arms. In fact I never resisted them, because while the pounds were piling on, I felt helpless, I even considered making myself sick again. But then I would imagine the excruciating pain that would cause. So I just gave up on losing weight and just allowed myself to get bigger. Secretly I admired and envied the other slim ladies. Often visualising what I would look like if only I managed to lose the extra pounds that had piled on.

To add insult to injury, during my pregnancy with Nathan Sean, my mum encouraged me to eat. She meant well. You see most people believe that for the unborn baby to grow, a pregnant woman has to eat for two, for herself and for the baby. I have since found out that this is only a myth. Your body adapts to the change caused by the pregnancy, and it absorbs more of the nutrients you eat. So your diet does not have to change drastically. Eating for two does not double your chances of having a bouncing baby, rather it will produce a big bouncing you, through weight gain, which will only increase your risk of pregnancy complications.

Without the correct knowledge of how much food intake I needed to increase during my pregnancy, I took advantage of the 'eating for two myth', coupled with my desire for food, it was an idea that was welcomed. I gladly indulged in whatever food I fancied, and succumbed to every food craving I had. Not only that, I would even force myself to eat when I was not feeling hungry.

Well of course you guessed it, the pounds piled on.

I remember feasting on Cumberland sausages and eggs for breakfast every morning. My husband and I once shared a whole chicken between us from Nando's and we scoffed it down without a second thought. Kentucky Fried Chicken was a favourite in our home; everybody around me knew that I found cooking my own meals too strenuous. 'Those were Happy Days'.

The unfortunate part of this tale is all the weight gain caused a medical condition known as pregnancy induced hypertension. Though it was only a mild form, it was enough to make me worry about my unborn child. I had to be induced, meaning I did not experience the natural onset of labour, or having my waters break naturally, something I was really looking forward to. The good news is we still welcomed a healthy bouncing baby boy weighing in at 6 pounds (2.8kg.)

After Nathan was born, I had got so used to the way I had been eating during the pregnancy that even after Nathan came home I continued. I remember when Nathan first came home from the hospital my family came over to our home to meet him. But after everyone left, Ko and I were not sure what to do with our new addition to the family. Nathan was very quiet, he just lay in his Moses Basket not crying or even squirming around. He just lay there, looking very content, all cute and cuddly, fast asleep. So Ko and I, not knowing what else to do, resorted to what we did best – yes eat. Though Ko was not affected at all. Every time he ate, I piled on the pounds. All that unhealthy eating added to the baby weight I had gained throughout the pregnancy, took its toll on my body and I weighed in at a staggering 13 stone (85 kg.)

Even though the weight kept piling on, there was never a point in my life that I was not trying to lose weight. I discovered yoyo dieting. I tried every diet that I heard about, including the Atkins diet, the fruit and vegetable only diet, Weight Watchers and Skinny Fibre. I even tried praying. There was only ever one prayer request from me, 'please pray for me to lose weight'. My pastors would often laugh at my prayer request. I now realise surely that there were probably better things to pray for other than for Gertrude to lose weight.

For years I tried different diets, but nothing seemed to work. The weight would fall off, but once I got tired of the diet, I would put the weight back on again. This carried on for a total of ten years. I would lose a stone (6 kgs) and then put a stone and a half (9 kgs.) back on again.

Throughout these years, I feel that I missed out on a whole chuck of my life, though I never avoided weighing scales. I was always aware of my weight readings. The only thing I avoided was the camera. I loathed having my picture taken.

Often I felt that I had to be humorous to cover up for my being overweight, that way I could be accepted and I thought people would not judge me but accept me because I made them laugh. I never made it a secret that I was unhappy with my weight though, I cried openly, I needed help.

But no one could help me, as they did not even take me seriously. Or maybe it was something I needed to sort out myself as an individual. I considered my being overweight had been caused by a form of addiction – food addiction. Unfortunately it was the most frowned upon entity I had ever come across. I believe and still do, that people who are addicted to drugs and alcohol receive more sympathy than those who are overweight, even more so than those who want to stop smoking.

I recall having a conversation with my brother-in-law, while seeking sympathy and genuine help to lose weight. He simply replied me, "just stop eating". How I wished it had been that simple. Unfortunately for him, he had mentioned that he was trying to stop smoking. So you can imagine how I felt about his response. I had equated his struggle to stop smoking with my struggle to lose weight. So imagine that statement coming from someone who was trying to stop smoking. My response to that reply was simply offering him the same help he had given me. "Just stop smoking". To which he bluntly replied "it was not the same, smoking is different". Hence my reason for believing that people who are trying to stop smoking receive a lot more sympathy.

I felt that people judged me instantly everywhere I went, because overweight people have a stigma attached to them. People just assume you are lazy and like eating the wrong food. But really – in my opinion – as mentioned before, I perceive it as an addiction to food. Even though I knew that eating greasy fried food is what had piled on those pounds, yet I could not seem to tear myself away from it. That packet of custard creams, all it takes is just popping one biscuit into my mouth, and before I know it the packet is empty, then the feelings of guilt take over.

The worst part is that food addiction is harder, because unlike substance abuse, where you can live without the substance, but with food, you need it to survive. Where do you draw the line? How do you find the balance? Unlike other addictions, which can be successfully hidden, food addiction cannot be hidden well, because your body will soon disclose the secret and take over your life.

Personally being overweight governed my life, I remember going to Southend-on-Sea in Essex. There is an Adventure island fun fair theme park right next to the sea, with all these amazing rides. I was excited and could not wait to get on one of the rides, the roller coaster. I was ready for the real deal; I wanted to feel the adrenaline rush I had heard people talk about every time they had been to a theme park. After waiting patiently in the long queues for what seemed like hours, my turn to enjoy the ride came. When my turn came I excitedly jumped into the coaster car. To my disappointment, the giant roller coasters safety bars wouldn't close, my thighs were already being squeezed so tightly against the bars. At that moment I thanked God I was dark skinned, at least no one would notice me blushing. Eventually the safety bar closed pinching my skin.

There were people screaming with excitement, yes I joined in the screaming but mine were screams of excruciating pain from where the safety bars were pinching the flesh in my thighs. After that nightmare, every time we went out to theme parks, I had to pretend I was too scared to go on any of the rides. Yet inside, I was dying to get on those rides.

The worst tale associated with my obese years was in 2007. That was the year that I not only got diagnosed with sciatica and kissed my nursing career goodbye; I had breathing problems too, and had to be prescribed a salbutamol asthma pump and steroids, despite being pregnant with my youngest son Ryan Shammah. He turned out to be very hyper and active. I have always blamed the steroids I had to take. During his pregnancy I also developed pregnancy induced hypertension a second time, only this time because I was classified as being clinically obese weighing in at 15 stone 7 pounds (100kg), it was a bit more severe, my legs were so swollen I could not walk unaided.

The doctor informed me I was heading for pre-eclampsia (a condition in pregnancy characterised by high blood pressure), I had to be induced at 38 weeks. I could have reduced my risk of getting these illnesses or avoided them all together if I had been at a healthy weight.

In my defence throughout the entire yo-yo dieting period, I was just trying to find a way to lose weight. The only problem was I got bored with the diets, because every time I tried a new diet, I became overly restrictive with my food intake and did not allow myself any treats. I would set goals for myself but never achieve them. I believed that for someone to be slim, they had to feel hungry all the time.

For the first time in my life I felt like a complete failure, an overwhelming sense of shame began to sweep over me. I knew I had to find myself somehow. I just didn't know where to start.

By the time 2013 came around, I was ready for a change. I somehow felt that year would be different for me, so in January 2013, like most people do, I made a New Year's resolution, to lose weight, and to somehow miraculously stumble on my destiny. Having decided enough was enough, I embarked on a weight loss plan, I remember weighing in at exactly 16 stone. But low and behold my pastor called for the whole church to go on a forty day fast, to pray and seek God without eating any food from six am to six pm.

That sounded easy enough. Yes I was determined to complete the forty days fast, so basically I ate nothing all day, but come six o'clock, I would not only eat my dinner, but I would eat breakfast and lunch too. My eating habits worsened with the fast, so I just got bigger and bigger. I had a very old set of scales at that time, which I could not rely on so I would only weigh myself when I visited my sister Irene. Really at first, I had no idea what I weighed. I've since learnt that is a no no; make it a golden rule to always know your weight.

I just fooled myself into believing I was maintaining the 16st weight I was before I started the fast. Though my clothes were getting tighter, I began making excuses for myself, I would convince myself I looked beautiful big, I just had to find clothes that suited me, (I never did). To me it always appeared as though the bigger the size was – especially from size 18 – the clothes somehow lost their shape. Then I didn't want the clothes anymore.

Shopping for clothes was something I absolutely loathed, I remember going shopping with my husband once, and a size 22 pair of trousers would not go past my thighs, I just burst into tears, my husband had to come into the ladies changing room to find out what had happened. From that day, I resorted to wearing leggings and baggy tops.

After the forty day fast, I knew I had put on weight, but kept promising myself I would start dieting tomorrow, but as one pastor said to me once… "Tomorrow never comes".

Chapter Four

Wake-up Call

Sure enough my tomorrow did not come until Sunday 3 June 2013. That is the day I received my wake up call, I remember the day so vividly. It was a Sunday afternoon after church. Everyone had been invited to my pastor's house for a barbeque. The weather was beautiful, the warm June sun was just right, not too hot, there was a cool breeze blowing, the sky was clear blue, not a cloud in sight, just perfect for a barbeque.

Well I arrived at my pastor's house to find the kitchen buzzing, already packed with women making salads and marinating the meat in preparation for the barbeque. Everyone was chatting away excitedly. I decided to make myself a cup of tea, after all I had skipped breakfast so felt I really deserved one. I even offered to make a cup for anyone else who might have wanted one. No one answered me, so I proceeded to make myself a hot drink.

Right next to the kettle was a plate full of freshly home baked cupcakes, they looked so scrumptious, and inviting, and I heard them call out to me Getty, Getty, not even in an English accent Gerty NO! It was definitely a Shona accent, one I understood so well, Getty, Getty. Who was I to resist that?

I excitedly answered the cupcakes call and helped myself to one, placed it on a plate. As I was about to sink my teeth in the cookie, carefully avoiding to drip any mouth juices as my mouth was already salivating in anticipation of tasting the warm, freshly home baked cupcake. Suddenly I was rudely interrupted, I say rudely because I could not wait to taste that cupcake. Sandra one of the other ladies from church asked me if we could share my cupcake, as she did not want to eat a full one.

Shivering with delicious horror at the thought of her request, I giggled. What! Share a freshly home baked cupcake, was that even legal? Certainly not in my world. So you can guess what my response was. Leaning over so no one would hear what I had to say, I pulled Sandra into a half tight hug, and whispered to her that I had no intention of sharing that cupcake with her or anyone else.

Well my response was met with some harsh words. These words changed my life forever. Despite my efforts to keep the conversation just between Sandra and me, Cleopatra's ears had somehow managed to catch my response. The words that carelessly rolled out of her mouth still ring in my ears till this day.

Allow me to introduce Cleopatra to you. She is one of the ladies from our church. Very well known for being liberal with her mouth, speaking out word's that should only be confined in her thoughts. Really what she had to say wasn't supposed to have bothered me judging from the description of her that I've just given, right? Well, she looked me straight in the eyes, disgust written all over her face, and said, "Look at you! Why are you eating things like cupcakes and cake? Can't you see that you just keep getting bigger and bigger, fatter and fatter? Your husband is going to leave you. You look more like Ko's mother than his wife". Those ice cold words echoed in my ears as they travelled all the way down and pierced my heart. I digested each word carefully and they felt like a stab wound, numb and cold.

Time seemed to stop for a moment, and I'm certain the room reduced in size and was squeezing the life out of me, I felt like I had no breath left. All I wished for was the ground to just open up and swallow me. I remember shivering involuntarily, as hot tears burned my eyelids threatening to roll down my cheeks, which were already burning with embarrassment.

The room went dead quiet; it was like everyone was judging me and they were all in total agreement with what had just been said. It was written all over their faces. No sympathy from any one at all. To make matters worse, this audience was waiting with anticipation for my reply.

A few hurtful things I could have answered Cleopatra, crossed my mind. I even visualised myself strangling her, but somehow all the muscles in my body had lost their ability to function. In what seemed like a decade later, I managed to place the cupcake back on the plate without even having taken a bit from it. I managed to sweep up what little dignity I had left and tear myself away from the kitchen and into the living room without having said a word. I had lost the ability to use my mouth. That wasn't all; with it I lost my appetite. There was such big lump stuck in my throat nothing could move it; it was permanently lodged there. My stomach churned, and I don't think I would have been able to keep any food down if I had tried to eat. At least I had enough respect for myself to walk away without having said a word.

Is this what it was going to take to get me to lose the weight that had robbed me of my joy for so many years…?

That's Ko and I at my biggest

And here two days before I started my lifestyle change

As I left my pastor's house later that evening, all I remember thinking was the sky didn't look so blue anymore. It was covered in grey clouds. I was blue instead. The only place I would find comfort now was my bed and certainly not even in a bag of Walkers Sensations Thai Sweet Chilli Crisps. I managed to avoid telling Ko the events that had transpired earlier that evening. I was not ready to retell them, even though I had played that scene a thousand times over in my head.

I pondered on what Cleopatra had said to me for the rest of that week, contemplating what I was going to do about my weight.

To make me feel better, I had a conversation with my husband and I repeated what Cleopatra had said. Though it was a bit exaggerated by my actions. I had to make my husband understand how deeply she had hurt me. Obviously my husband tried to console me by telling me that he loved me no matter how I looked. The sad part was I wanted to believe him. But in fact I didn't believe him. I had always thought that secretly he loathed the extra weight I had piled on over the years. I wasn't exactly the woman he had fallen in love with and married thirteen years ago. Even though he had never mentioned it, the weight must have bothered him I'm sure. But he had to play his part as the loving and supporting husband. Yes for better or worse, right? So his words were supposed to soothe me and make me feel better, but to my surprise, they didn't. I realised that whether I believed him or not, did not matter.

Nothing it seemed could take the hurting feeling away. Or so I thought. Burning anger rose within me, I wanted to wallow in self-pity over my helplessness. Lost in my own thoughts I did not even hear the rest of my husband's comforting lies.

Suddenly all the emotions I had been carrying around with me for years, emotions of being a failure, all the setbacks, feeling lost and having no sense of direction, a longing to be accepted by other people and including being overweight came rushing back and resurfaced. I realised I had no sense of identity. Jackie Chan's movie *Who Am I* crossed my mind. Who was I, what was my purpose here on earth? Was it just to be a wife, a good fat one at that and a mother and end there?

Those emotions had evoked unpleasant memories of all my failures. I could not stop the tears rolling down my cheeks. This wasn't even about my husband or poor Cleopatra. It was then that I realised and remembered the true meaning of the following words written by Dr Robert Anthony, that, "when you blame others you give up your power to change". Cleopatra had just taken it upon herself to highlight that I was just getting bigger, a fact I already knew. I had entertained this fact for far too long now. This was an issue that had been hiding and was now rearing its ugly head AGAIN. That is why In Epi Mabika's words, "it is very important to make life decisions before life makes those decisions for you, you either live by design or by default". Life was forcing me to make a decision now. If that was the case, then I was going to do it my way, I had to start by accepting and taking full responsibility of my life, and stop blaming others, and making excuses.

Surprisingly, with all those emotions racing in my head, an unexplainable feeling of overwhelming calmness seemed to blanket those emotions and settled in my heart. It was as if these emotions were initiating some positive self-correcting attitudes in my thought process.

There was war raging in my mind. Instantly I came to the realisation that the battlefield is in the mind. There were strong emotions of fear. What if I failed again? But with every negative emotion or barrier, I had a positive answer for it. It was as if I had reached a point where I had the power to shape my life. Before me were two roads, I could accept the feelings of defeat or I could fight them head on and instead defeat them. If I could win this battle in my mind then my job was half done.

I began to see myself in a different light. This was my battle, so I chose to face and fight it head on. It was time to confront those demons once and for all, and with it find my purpose in this life. Losing weight could be the key I needed to unlock and fulfil my destiny.

If I was going to lose weight, this time it had to be for me. That day I made a promise to myself. I was going to lose weight and lose it for good. Not only lose it, this time I had to do it the healthy way, and with it find my destiny. Losing weight was only the starting point.

It all started with a decision. I made a choice that day to change my lifestyle and start to live a healthy life. Images of how I would look when I reached my goal seemed to cloud my mind, and that picture changed my perception of the situation I had seemingly wondered into. The magic key that would unlock my destiny was perception. Your perception of a situation will determine the outcome of that situation.

The sound of Ko's voice startled me; I had been so focused on this new lease of life I had just discovered. He was still trying to convince me that he loved me just the way I was. I looked into his kind eyes and could see genuine concern written all over his face, which reminded me why I had married him.

My face broke into a smile and through the tears, I just managed to say, "I know you love me." I was not ready to let him in on my new secret. Not just yet anyway. I had to test the waters first and with time he would see for himself. I would let him see for himself, as the saying goes action does speak louder than words. 'Sometimes you do not need to tell people your dreams, just show them'.

Thank God for a new day. The following week didn't seem so gloomy. After all I had settled the raging war in my mind and I felt quite confident about the new journey that lay before me. The previous week had been a new dawn for me. I had discovered a secret weapon, everyone had the power to shape and rewrite their own destiny, and I grabbed my opportunity with both hands. As a dear friend of mine once said, "you only have one life so live it."

Something was different this time, Cleopatra's brutal honesty had unlocked a part of me I felt had never been explored before, the part that had been craving to be exposed, was I now treading on unchartered territory?

Was this the part of my life that was waiting, lying idle, and waiting for me to discover it? I felt like I had been given another chance to turn my life around. I was holding onto that second chance for dear life.

Chapter Five

Lifestyle Change

Often I had prayed that if God helped me lose weight to my desired healthy goal weight, I would endeavour to maintain it. Here was a chance to do just that. That evening, sitting on the edge of my bed, I took out a note pad from my dresser and in it I wrote the following prayer, Philippians 4:13, 'I can do all things through Christ who Strengthens me', and Psalm 37:5

'Commit your way to the Lord, trust also in Him and He will bring it to pass'.

Believe it or not, I had prayed these prayers before, but something was different this time. I was tired of being the biggest ugliest sister, which made me look years older than my sisters. I am actually the youngest of the three sisters. Having beautiful sisters just makes it harder. I was tired of being trapped in this fat body, period.

After praying, I knew I had to be practical and devise a plan. Sometimes, we Christians become so spiritual, we are neither good to man or beast. I had to be practical. I had to let go of this comfort zone I had become so accustomed to and yet it had brought me so much pain. Neale Donald Walsch put it beautifully when he said, "Life begins at the end of your comfort zone". Yes I had definitely reached the end of my comfort zone.

So my mind began to take me on a journey. A picture began to form in my head of how I would look once I reached my goal weight, how the clothes would look on me. I believed beyond doubt that I could do it. So I set my final goal weight, believing I would achieve it. You see, Dan O'Deen couldn't have said it better than this,

"Faith is like the Wi-Fi, invisible but it has the power to connect you to what you desire".

Next, I needed an action plan, so I turned to WeightWatchers, I had tried them before and lost 3 stone (19 kgs) on it, so I knew it worked. It was the only weight loss plan, which had sort of worked.

Let me explain how the plan works; WeightWatchers is a weight loss programme, which basically encourages healthy eating, and portion control, as well as exercise. You can either follow the programme online or attend a weekly meeting. Every meeting has a leader who basically weighs you every week. You can also discuss any areas you may be struggling with your weight loss at the meetings or privately with the leader.

The best part which worked for me about Weight Watchers is I didn't know how much I needed to eat. How do you find the balance? How much food do I need to eat to remain healthy and not starve myself, because the formula for weight loss is simply to consume fewer calories than your body burns. That's the dilemma, how do you work out how many calories to consume.

So I used the Weight Watchers formula. They calculate the right amount of calories or food a person can have, ensuring they reach a balance of nutrition without exceeding their daily recommended limit of calories. According to a person's gender, height, and weight, Weight Watchers calculates how many calories you have to eat in the form of points. Every portion of food is assigned a points value, for example a slice of bread is assigned two points, a teaspoon of Lurpak butter is one point. At the end of the day you add up all the points assigned to the food you eat and add them up. The idea is to not exceed your allocated points for the day. Basically that part of my weight loss was inspired by Weightwatchers.

After having worked out how much food I could eat in a day. I went and purchased a set of digital scales to replace my old useless ones. When I jumped on the scale, I weighed in at a staggering 16 stone 13 pounds (107 kgs) my biggest weight ever. I was carrying nearly 17 stone on my 5 foot 4 inches frame, it was the reason why I was suffering with sciatic pain in my left thigh, and the migraines I suffered with nearly every week.

That weigh in was not going to deter me. All right yes, I admit I was completely overwhelmed by how much weight I had to lose to be at a healthy weight. But Instead of feeling sorry for myself, I decided those emotion's would became the strength I needed to face my weight loss battle.

Inspired by my previous experience at Weight Watchers, and equipped with the knowledge I had from reading about healthy eating and exercise, I created my own weight loss programme by doing what worked for me. The reason I looked and studied other weight loss programmes was because I learnt from Alfred Sheinwold's quote that, "you need to learn all you can from the mistakes of others, so you won't have to make them all yourself". The mistake I made with Weight Watchers before was that I became dependent on my leader, as if I was losing weight for her. But soon I found excuses not to attend the meetings. If I had a bad week or if I wanted to overindulge I would just tell myself, that I would miss the meeting and attend the following week, the following week turned into weeks, then it became months and before I knew it, it turned into years.

That was my downfall with Weight Watchers. This time, I had to be accountable to me and no one else. I was doing this not for my Weight Watchers leader but for me.

The next important step was to just take one day at a time. That was all I needed. I was certain that I was on the right road. I was well-equipped for my journey. As Orison Swett Marden was known for saying, "when we are sure that we are on the right road there is no need to plan our journey too far ahead. No need to burden ourselves with doubts and fears as to the obstacles that may bar our progress". Slowly every day I incorporated changes. I wasn't in a hurry as I was not looking for a quick fix. It had taken me nearly seventeen years to put on this weight, and there was no way it was going to fall off overnight. Wasn't it Jim Rohn who said, "Some things you must do every day, eating seven apples one night instead of one a day isn't going to get the job done"?

Slowly our eating habits changed, I didn't want to alienate myself from the rest of my family by cooking separate meals, so I started cooking healthy meals for everyone to enjoy, and we replaced unhealthy snacks with healthy ones. Being overweight does not only affect adults, sadly it can affect children as well. Statistics show that around one in every five children aged between ten and eleven are overweight.

Most parents do not realise that overweight children will grow into overweight adults. As a parent I decided that it was never too late or too early to introduce my children to healthy eating and a more active lifestyle. Besides, research shows that children who achieve a healthy weight tend to be fitter, healthier, and concentrate better at school. They are also more self-confident.

Above all a healthier lifestyle will reduce health problems later on in life. I wanted to be a good role model for my children by showing them how it is done, as children learn what they live rather than from what they are told. If you portray living a more active lifestyle as being fun, they will want to join in. So I encouraged my husband and my children to come walking with me instead of riding in the car all the time. In turn I would join them while playing in the park. I found this to be a free form of entertainment the whole family could join in and have fun.

Another important rule I learnt was never to set boundaries for myself, remember, this was not a diet, and I called it a lifestyle change. This was going to be my style of eating until death do us apart.

The difference between diets and lifestyle change is; lifestyle change is gradual sustainable realistic changes that you make towards your eating habits, and include being more active as part of your daily routine. You have to unlearn your old eating habits and introduce new healthy ones. Human beings are creatures of habit and routine, that's why introducing the new habits has to be a gradual process. Once these new habits are learnt, and replace our old eating habits, it won't be easy to unlearn them.

Now, with a diet and most weight loss programmes out there, you can only be on them for a short time, and you soon get tired of them because they are overly restrictive and boring. How long can you drink tasteless milkshakes for? Or eat ready-made foods that have no spices and flavour added to them. I certainly do not enjoy taking medication even if it's to help me lose weight. Statics show that an individual is prone to go back to their old eating habits when they are on a diet because they soon get bored, which results in all their weight going straight back on.

The greatest gift you have in life is being yourself. Create your own plan that works for you. As long as it is healthy and you are eating until you feel satisfied, then it will work better for you.

Above all, I had to be committed to this lifestyle change. I would occasionally allow myself treats, and did not overly restrict my favourite foods. Nutritionist Joy Bauer, in her book entitled *The Joy Fit Club: Cookbook,* mentions that, "think of weight loss as a 90 to 10 balance, eating healthy 90 per cent of the time and cheat 10 per cent of the time". I have this article posted on my fridge door to serve as a reminder.

To help me remain focused on my goal, I would often visualise how I would look when I finally reached my goal weight. This made me desire it even more. I made sure that I always rewarded my efforts by allowing myself treats. My treats did not only consist of food. I bought myself designer handbags or shoes, or designer sunglasses, to acknowledge my progress.

I would spend hours reading about nutrition and exercise, how incorporating them would benefit me health wise. The bigger picture was; it wasn't just about losing weight, the health benefits were numerous and by far outweighed the weight loss benefits. I came to the conclusion that weight loss was a bonus, being healthy was more important.

In my note pad, I made a list of all my favourite foods, and compared them with the healthy options. One by one I scratched out all the unhealthy options, and made a separate column for treats. I swapped my favourite cake with a banana, thank God for bananas. My typical meal would consist of; for breakfast a bowl of bran flakes with semi-skimmed milk and a cup of tea; for lunch egg salad and for dinner vegetables and steak – got to have some meat. When I got tired of cereals I turned to my beloved toast and butter. I tried to keep my food choices exciting by trying out new recipes as well.

To keep active, I started walking, and that became my favourite hobby. Going to the gym was not an option for me. For starters I could not afford a gym membership, and because I was classified as clinically obsess, I would be too embarrassed to be seen in a gym and would feel too conscious of my every move. I would have also found all the slimmer people too intimidating, so walking seemed to appeal more to me. The best part, it was free. I loved breathing in the fresh air and enjoyed looking at the scenery around me, the big beautiful houses that I imagined living in one day. It seemed to make my decision to walk a lot more enjoyable.

As I still suffered from sciatica, I had to start at a very slow pace. In the beginning, I started out walking for four miles, five days a week. It would take me one and a half hours to walk the four miles. I would never over exert myself, but began walking at a very comfortable pace. I would walk for five days come rain wind or sunshine.

One morning it was raining cats and dogs, and I still went out for my daily walk. Thirty minutes later, I was surprised to find Ko had followed me in his car begging me to come out of the rain and into the car. His voice sounded shocked but it was very stern, as if the idea of me walking in the rain was absurd. But I was not going to let a bit of rain stop me from reaching my goals. Dolly Parton put it this way, "if you want the rainbow, you have to tolerate the rain". I was determined. I avoided looking him in his eyes just in case my resolve crumbled. Eventually, he gave up and left me walking in the rain.

For the first few months, the results were very encouraging, every week the pounds fell off. I was losing weight steadily; I always lost an average of 2 pounds (0.5 to 1kg) a week. I would weigh myself first thing before breakfast at nine o'clock in the morning, on a Wednesday every week, wearing just my pants and bra. The reading on the scale had to be accurate. Everything I did was documented. The reason for documenting every weight loss or gain was so that I could always revisit it and see why I had lost or gained that week. I would take pictures of my weigh in sessions and of my meals as well.

To keep me motivated and interested in my new adventure, I started a chat group on What's App, social media, and added my mum and sisters on it. Together we shared weight loss tips to keep us motivated. Every day we would post what we would have had for our meals and any exercise. It helped to keep us accountable to our new life style.

Even on days when my mum and sisters gave up and stopped posting their meals on the social media, I continued, I had too much at stake and nothing was going to stop me, or so I thought, until one morning, after losing 3 stone (19 kg), I hit the dreaded weight loss plateau.

A weight loss plateau is when after a period of successful weight loss your body gets used to the new routine you have introduced it to, and just stops responding, despite all your hard work, your body works even harder against you to hold on to the weight you are desperately trying to lose. This minor setback was not going to deter me. I had to think of new ways to get the weight falling off again.

Thank God for technology, instead of crying about it or even giving up, I consulted the Internet, and read that when you hit a weight loss plateau, you need to trick your body by either increasing your calorie intake or reducing it while increasing your daily work outs or exercises.

Following the advice I had read on the Internet, I increased my walking distance to five miles, I needed the xtra push. It would take me two hours at first, but gradually I built up on speed and now it only takes me one hour twenty-five minutes.

Having increased my walking distance, it was not long before the pounds started falling off again.

After losing four stone (25kgs), I was so desperate for people to notice that I was losing weight, but for days, weeks, even months, my weight loss went unnoticed. My husband would often simply reply whenever I asked him if I had lost weight, "Continue"! My friends and family would say, "when we can notice it you won't have to ask".

This never deterred me, I could see the figures reducing on the scales week after week and that was good enough for me, besides I had the rest of my life to put my new lifestyle change into practice.

Finally, after losing five stone (31kgs), I didn't have to ask anyone if they could notice my weight loss. Everyone began to notice. The best part was when my friends and most people who knew me when I was overweight were not able to recognise me when I walked past them. I remember my sons piano teacher walked right past me in Brentwood High Street, Essex. I had to run after her and introduce myself. The look on her face when she recognised me was priceless.

I still go out on my walks and often people stop in their cars just to let me know that they have been watching me since I started. I'm often reminded of the big brown tracksuit bottoms I used to wear. But it's the smiles on their faces when they all congratulate me on how far I have come. One lady said to me, "you were slow and fat when you first started." That just put a smile on my face, remembering how hard I had found walking my first mile, I was panting heavily all the way. Now it's just a distant memory with a satisfied customer.

Chapter Six

Beauty for Ashes

One year later on 9 June 2014, I reached my goal weight of 10 stone 10 pounds (68kg). I had imagined this day for a very long time so you can imagine the excitement I felt when the numbers on the scale read 10 stone 10 pounds (68 kgs). Finally I had reached the weight I had desired for so long. A desire that went from being an impossibility to a possibility and eventually became a reality. All I could manage to do was fall on my knees and cry, tears of joy. All the hard work, determination and persistence had finally paid off.

To celebrate my achievements, I made sure that when we went away on holiday, I went on every ride at the Chessington Theme Park Resort. I had to make up for all the years I made excuses to not go on those rides. This time around, the screams from me were of genuine delightful excitement, thrill and pleasure from the adrenaline rush.

I had become so used to living with this pain in my heart. A longing for something I once believed was beyond my reach. I had felt weighted down and was very self-conscious. When I was fat I used to wish that I would fit in, I just longed to be normal. Whenever I went to a party, all I worried about was 'what am I going to eat next'? Now when I go to a party, I'm too busy showing off my new dance moves to worry about food, because I'm so comfortable in my body. I've also developed a new passion for fashion.

Sometimes I'm certain, my husband wishes I were overweight again, as keeping up with the latest fashion trends is expensive. I have definitely become more daring, wearing make-up and jewellery; I regularly treat myself to facials, manicures and pedicures.

The most amazing part of my journey is I have discovered the power and freedom to express who I really am and conquer my low self-esteem issues which trail back to when I was 13 years old, when I felt the bitter taste of being rejected. The excuse I had been holding onto for my low self-esteem.

It was my first year in high school, on the first day. Sarah, Pamela and I had been friends since second grade, but when we went to high school, Pamela was sadly sent away to boarding school, leaving just Sarah and I to be best friends, right? But that was not the case. On the first day of High School, Sarah made new friends quite quickly and together they decided I did not fit in their new circles. They decided they would be the new popular girls in school. Sadly I did not qualify to be in their group. She was the only best friend I had ever had for seven years. Yet she stood there listening while her new best friend called me names.

At that time I never actually realised how deeply wounded I had been, but throughout the years this experience of being rejected lead to feelings of inadequacy, insecurity and above all a longing to be accepted by everyone and never be rejected again.

This even affected most of my adult life. Even though I forgave Sarah for what she did to me, the effects of that rejection had taken its roots. That experience had dented my self-confidence. I was always so apologetic for everything because the thought of someone not liking me would often haunt me for days, sometimes even making me feel I was sorry that I had ever been born.

If I had a decision to make, I would first consult five different people before making a decision, so that no one would judge me about the decisions I had made. I was so overly sensitive, so I would analyse people's behaviours and question why they behaved in that way towards me. I never felt I was good enough, even when other people paid me a compliment, I found it hard to accept those compliments. Worst of all I wanted to be liked by everybody.

All that has changed for me now, which made this journey more interesting than any other, because on this journey I discovered who the real Gertrude was, and I fell in love with her. I have a newfound confidence and everyone has noticed the change in me. Since losing weight, I now realise I do not need permission from anyone to express myself and I have come to the powerful realisation that not everyone in life is going to like me, but that's okay. In Steve Maraboli's words, "when I accept myself, I am freed of the burden of needing you to accept me". The late Maya Angelou also confirmed the way I feel when she said, "you alone are enough, you have nothing to prove to anybody". Now, I'm living life on my own terms.

I don't think negatively about my life anymore, I have no regrets either. Aubrey O'Day quoted it so well when he said, "You can never regret anything you do in life. You kind of have to learn the lesson from whatever the experience is and take it with you on your journey forward". Everything that happens in life happens for a reason.

My story is not a one sided story, it's not every fat girls story, but it's my story. It's the best thing that happened to me. As beautifully quoted by Helen Keller, the famous blind poet, "The best and most beautiful things in the world cannot be seen or even touched, they must be felt with the heart". That describes the joy I feel – pure joy – beauty radiating from the inside. Knowing I look good on the outside and I'm healthy on the inside gives me all the confidence I need to tackle whatever life may throw at me. Every morning I wake up celebrating my life. The world is my oyster. I take pride in how far I have come, and I'm not about to stop celebrating.

The ashes in my life, which consisted of being overweight, having no sense of self-worth, and no ambition have turned into something beautiful. So I don't focus on the past, though I'm grateful for my struggle because it was integral in forming whom I am today. I realise that I needed those ashes to find the strength that lay hidden away. I stopped chasing the fad diets and trying to please other people, then the real Gertrude caught up with me.

I have a new definition for life; 'life is about making choices, facing your fears and building your dreams'. It's certainly not As Epi Mabika confirmed, "downgrading your dreams to match your reality, but certainly about upgrading your faith to match your destiny". Knowing what you want is the most important step you can take towards finding your destiny.

Losing weight just made me realise that your destiny is not out of your control, you definitely have a choice in the matter. Don't just sit there believing 'whatever will be will be'. I dare you to chase your dreams and be a go-getter.

Now that I have found the missing puzzle to complete my destiny, I know exactly what career path I'm going to take, one that Rob Hill Sr describes so well, "My goal is to build a life I don't need a vacation from". Stop me if you can…

Recent picture of me at my desired healthy goal weight

Chapter Seven

Conclusion

I hope you have been inspired by my journey. As you embark on your own weight loss journey here is my personal *ABC Plan* and 'quick reference' tips to losing weight, and keeping it off for good, that you can apply to help you achieve your goals.

The ABC of Weight Loss

Remember as the saying goes, stay cool if plan 'A' doesn't work the alphabet has 25 more letters.

ccept and acknowledge you are overweight, don't wait for someone to point it out to you. You cannot lose weight for someone else; you need to lose weight for yourself. When you have decided that you want to lose weight, do not avoid the responsibility of how your body looks by making excuses, one of my favourite ones was, "I am big boned". You don't put on weight without working hard at it. If you do not like the way you look and feel, then you are accountable and only you can change it. If you don't like something, change it. The late Maya Angelou couldn't have said it better when she said, "If you can't change it, change your attitude".

elieve you can and you are halfway there. When you believe something, you start expecting it. "Anything the mind of man can conceive and believe it can achieve", is one of Napoleon Hill's hallmark expressions. When you do not believe you can achieve something, you limit yourself, and you build barriers in your mind, disarming yourself of the ability to achieve anything. As the saying goes, "forget all the reasons why it won't work and believe all the reasons why it will work and expect to win".

ommit to the lifestyle change. Do not be overly restrictive in terms of the type of foods you can eat, make realistic changes to your diet that you know you can stick to for the rest of your life. Incorporate your favourite foods into your food plan. Kenneth Blanchard summed it up so well when he said, “When interested in doing something, you do it only when convenient, but when committed, you accept no excuses, only results”.

etermination is the gateway to any success. Lewis Pugh inspired me when he said, “there is nothing as powerful as a made up mind”. Yes you will meet obstacles on the way, but view everyday as an opportunity to start again if you failed yesterday; better yet view the next meal as an opportunity to start again. Persevere towards your goal no matter how difficult. Life always offers you a second chance, it’s called tomorrow. “When obstacles arise you change your direction to reach your goal, you do not change your decision to get there”, is one of Zig Ziglar’s quotes that sum determination so well. Another one of Winston Churchill’s quotes that define determination well is, “success is not final, failure is not fatal it is the courage to continue that counts”.

xercise is vital not only for weight loss; it is recommended that all adults should aim for at least 30 minutes of moderate intensity physical activity on at least five days of the week. It does not have to be intense to start off with; you can start by just walking for half an hour a day. Weight loss is simply ensuring that your calorie intake is less than your total daily calories burned through physical activity. Increase your physical activity and gradually increase the intensity. Besides, the new physical and activity guidelines state that an active lifestyle can lower your risk of early death from a variety of causes and also keep you looking younger. Scientists have also confirmed that walking fights age related illnesses.

ocus on your goal. Once you have decided on your long-term healthy ideal goal weight, write it down. Catherine Pulsifer once said that, "you must stay focused on the end result to achieve your goals". One of the challenges I faced through my weight loss journey was people telling me I had lost enough weight, before reaching my ideal goal weight. I did not let this deter me, because I had visualised myself at my ideal goal weight, I knew what I wanted to achieve. Buy a dress in the size you want to eventually be as a reminder of your long-term goal.

radual sustainable weight loss is what you should aim for. Aim to lose at least 0.5 kg to 1 kg which is 1 to 2 pounds a week. The best way is not to lose weight too fast, if you lose more than a kilogram or two pounds a week, you may lose muscle tissue rather than fat. Don't be in too much of a hurry to see results and don't let slow progress deter you or discourage you. Some people quit due to slow progress, but remember even slow progress is progress; an inch of movement is still progress.

itting the dreaded weight loss plateau is inevitable. A weight loss plateau can be very frustrating. Having a stretch where your weight loss slows down or the scale's don't move is quite common and a natural part of weight loss. Just keep in mind that if you continue your new lifestyle change, you will eventually start losing again. Focus on other aspects of eating healthy, like the new burst of energy you now have. Even if you don't get an effective weigh loss result, you are still gaining healthy effects in your body.

nteresting; keep your journey interesting; one of the reasons most people give up on their weight loss journey is because they soon get bored. Keep your weight loss journey interesting by trying out new healthy recipes the whole family can enjoy. Be adventurous and creative too. Create new healthy recipes; creativity will certainly keep you committed. Discover new routes you can walk, by taking a different path or going in the opposite direction. As you are walking make an effort to notice your surroundings. Join a dance group like Zumba; be more daring.

Just Do It. "The most effective way to get something done, is to just do it", is a quote by Amelia Earhart. Time spent thinking about something takes away the time you actually have to do it. Take action, as the saying goes, 'action always beats intention'. Stop making excuses, or wishing, or even dreaming about a slimmer healthier you, today just start doing it. "A year from now you will wish you had started today," is quote that will inspire anyone; it is attributed to Karen Lamb the author of *I Felt My Wings*. You might not have all the answers, its ok. Start even before you are ready. Sometimes, especially when you have a lot of weight to lose, it can seem very daunting and failure runs through your mind before you even start, but in Robert Kiyosaki's words, "if you try hard to avoid failing, you will also avoid success".

now what you want then desire it. Knowing what you want will help you decide on your final healthy goal weight. Then when you've decided on your final healthy weight, desire it! Dallin H. Oakes summed up knowing your desires so well when he said, "desires dictate our priorities, priorities shape our choices and choices determine our actions". Dr Philip C. McGraw in his book entitled *Life Strategies,* states that, "the most you will ever get is what you ask for. If you don't even know what it is that you want, then you cannot even ask for it. You also won't even know if you get there." Identifying and knowing your desires will help you make better choices that will direct you towards your goals.

earn to unlearn your old habits. Human beings are creature of habit. John Foreyt, in his article on *'Mechanisms and prevention of Obesity'*, says that, "many people are sceptical about changing their eating habits because they have grown accustomed to eating or drinking the same foods and there is a fear of the unknown or trying something new". But one of the things that is detrimental in your weight loss journey is old eating habits. Especially the ones we picked up from childhood, one of them is the 'cleaning your plate' thing. It was always a rule in my mother's house, to show that you enjoyed the food; I've learnt that parents don't always know best. Just because we have always done something a certain way, does not make it right. Learn new healthy habits, with time the new learned behaviours will overtake the old ones. You will find by the time you do get to your destination (that's your goal weight); the new healthy eating lifestyle will be hard to change as you will be so used to your new way of eating.

otivation. Keeping yourself motivated is crucial during your journey, get help from friends and family; surround yourself with people on the same mission as you. Start a chat group with friends to exchange ideas such as cooking recipes, or ways to keep you more active. Collect inspirational stories of people who have lost the same amount of weight you aiming to lose, and refer to them often. Involve your whole family in the lifestyle change, so they eat the same meals as you, that way your whole family will be healthy. Keep reminding yourself why you want to lose weight.

Nothing is impossible. "It always seems impossible until it's done", is a quote attributed to the late Nelson Mandela. Since I started my weight loss journey, if I had got a penny every time I was told I would never fit into a size 10 dress, it is impossible, I would be a very rich woman. If you put your mind to it, it is not impossible, yes even if you are a black woman. Francois de La Rochefoucauld summed it up so well when he said, "nothing is impossible, there are ways that lead to everything, and if we had sufficient will we should always have sufficient means. It is often merely for an excuse that we say things are impossible".

verweight. Remember being overweight is a choice. You may not feel that being overweight is a problem, but if you understood the health risks you might be inspired to lose weight. And literally, as quoted by Epi Mabika, "sometimes you don't feel the weight of something you've been carrying until you feel the weight of its release".

ursuit. In your pursuit of a healthier, slimmer you, don't forget to just enjoy your journey and have fun. Losing weight should not be a chore, and certainly is not about depriving yourself of the foods you love or strict diets and limitations, but rather an exciting journey of exploring and rediscovering a healthier you, who is beautiful on the inside and out.

uitting is for losers. A new weight loss survey from the United Kingdom found that nearly half of all dieters quit within a month of starting their diet. The reason I did not quit and succeeded with my weight loss was my approach. I recommend a lifestyle change and advocate changes to your eating and exercise plan that you can actually live with for the rest of your life. "If at any point you feel like quitting, think about why you started," said Epi Mabika. Overall in Bob Proctor's words, "be like a postage stamp – stick to it until you get there". Besides, quitters never win.

ecord your Journey. Document your progress no matter how small or insignificant. At the beginning of your journey, write down your reasons for wanting to lose weight and keep referring to them. This will help keep you motivated to continue on weeks when you do not lose weight. Keeping track of your progress can actually help you by bringing to your attention mistakes you might be making, or alert you when you hit a plateau in your progress and in turn help you improve your results. At the end of your journey you can look back and see how far you have come.

Set yourself an action plan. This will help you decide on the steps you will take to reach your goal. Start by setting yourself a realistic healthy goal weight. What form of exercise you will incorporate to become more active. Monitor your old and new eating habits. I did not realise how many needless calories I was consuming until I started to take an account of my eating habits. Also plan your meals in advance so you won't get caught with your hand in the cookie jar. Always have a healthy snack, preferably fruit, handy in your bag at all times, to minimise straying away from your new eating plan in case there is temptation. As the saying goes, "If you fail to plan, plan to fail". Always evaluate your eating habits.

reats are a must have. Allow yourself a treat at least one day every week, everyone likes a treat occasionally, so why not. Successful weight loss is eating healthy 90 per cent of the time, and cheating 10 per cent of the time. But remember to eat reasonably whilst cheating. Research has found that treating yourself (sensibly) while losing weight cannot only help you achieve greater weight loss; it also helps you stay motivated and eliminates binging. If you crave something unhealthy and it's not a cheat day, then share it or halve it.

nique. You are different in your own way, do what works for you. For example, I was not comfortable going to the gym, so I opted for walking instead, as I could easily fit it into my daily routine. It was a refreshing alternative to complicated aerobic routines, but most importantly it's free. On the other hand my sister Eunice was and still is obsessed with going to the gym, at the end of the day we both got the results we desired. Epi Mabika summed it up well when she said, "live life on your own terms: Life-By-design".

isualise yourself at your goal weight. Walt Disney said, "if you can dream it, you can do it". The vision of a slimmer you will create a burning desire to see your vision become a reality, and this burning desire will be key in achieving your goal, because once you've seen it, you will want it and if you want it, you will find a way to make it happen. Dr. Cindy Trimm in her book entitled, *'Commanding Your Morning'*, puts it beautifully when she quoted a friend who told her that '...your feet can never take you where your mind has never been'.

eigh yourself at least once every week. Invest in a good reliable digital scale. I recommend a set of Weight Watchers scales. Keep a log of your weight loss to monitor your progress. As well as weighing yourself weekly, take body measurements using a tape measure and measure your waist, bust, chest, calves, upper arms and hips. There will be days when all your hard work won't be noticeable on the scales. Seeing the same number week after week can be disheartening and might even make you want to give up altogether. That's when you can always turn to your body measurements, trust me, this will be a useful way to track your weight loss. Never assume or judge how much you weigh by your clothes, I noticed that your clothes grow big with you and lose weight with you. Do not become overly obsessed about the numbers on the scale either, rather focus on becoming healthier. Jack Dixon was attributed with saying, "If you focus on results you will never change, if you focus on change and the actions that produce results you will get results".

tra factor. The difference between ordinary and 'Xtraordinary' is that little 'Xtra'. Push yourself until you get results. What comes easy won't last, and what lasts won't come easy. I came to discover after watching *Britain's got Talent* that the human body is very flexible and is capable of doing much more than we give it credit for, even in terms of exercise. You just have to convince your mind that you can do it. Remember – No pain No Gain. As rightfully quoted by Vince Lombardi, "The only place where success comes before work is in the dictionary". Also remember the saying 'the best things in life don't come cheap'.

o-yo diets. Research shows that most women have no problem shedding weight; the hard part is keeping the weight off for good. These are the results that yo-yo dieting produces. Yo-yo dieting is term coined by Dr Kelly D. Brown; it refers to successfully losing weight in the initial stages only to put it back on again (like a yo-yo goes up and down). Good weight loss results can be achieved quite quickly, but they are short lived, and they only produce temporary results, they are more like a temporary fix, which can be very discouraging. Apart from that, some studies suggest that yo-yo dieting can increase the risk of certain health problems. Change your lifestyle to help you adapt to healthy eating and exercise, that's the only way to get effective weight loss results that last while reaping the health effects.

eal without knowledge is very dangerous, educate yourself, read about healthy eating and exercise. When I first decided I wanted to lose weight nearly seventeen years ago, I had no knowledge about how to lose weight the healthy way and maintain it; I resorted to self-harming, and actually believed that was the only way. If only I had done my research properly, I would not have an ulcer today. Epi Mabika is attributed with saying, "in the age of information, ignorance is a choice". There are lots of places where you can get information on healthy eating and exercise, make use of them, most of them are only a click away.

Tips to Lose Weight

- Fall in love with fruit. Most fruits are naturally low in fat, sodium and calories; none have cholesterol. They are guaranteed to keep hunger at bay.
- Eat three square meals every day and don't skip meals, as this will only make you feel hungry and you will keep thinking about food.
- Eating foods that contain a lot of fibre will keep you feeling full for longer.
- Limit fast food and takeaways to once a week, as these tend to be high in fat or sugar and salt. If you must have takeaways choose the

children's meals or share your adult meals. Try and eat a home cooked meal at least five days a week.

- Don't be overly restrictive on eating your favourite food. If you fancy it, have it in moderation.
- If you must drive to work, park farther away so you can walk the rest of the way, as Tesco says 'every little helps'.
- Avoid eating within three hours of going to bed, as going to bed full reduces the efficiency of the digestive system. And don't eat after dinner – even snacking – brush your teeth after you've eaten dinner.
- Use Skimmed milk instead of full fat milk.
- Grill, steam, boil or bake rather than fry your food.
- Reduce carbohydrates, increase foods that are high in fibre and always include proteins and vegetables in your weight loss plans.
- Spice up your vegetables or add chillies, to boost the flavour so they are not boring.
- Drink plenty of water instead of juices or fizzy drinks; most people sometimes confuse thirst with hunger. Research has shown that it is advisable to drink at least eight glasses of water every day. Take regular sips throughout the day.

- Stock your kitchen with healthy food, such as ready to eat snacks.
- While cooking, chew some sugar free gum to avoid eating whilst cooking, and if you have children, avoid becoming a bin by eating their leftovers, or even your husband's.
- Acknowledging your weight loss progress is vital, especially in the form of treats, but treats don't always have to be in the form of food. They can also come in the form of pampering yourself – a new hairstyle or a new pair of shoes.

'Bon voyage – Enjoy'!

ND - #0141 - 080726 - C0 - 197/132/6 - PB - 9781784561482 - Gloss Lamination